DISCLAIMER

Please note that the publisher of this instructional book is NOT RESPONSIBLE in any manner whatsoever for any injury which may occur by reading and/or following the instructions herein.

It is essential that before following any of the activities, physical or otherwise, herein described, the reader or readers should first consult his or her physician for advice on whether or not the reader or readers should embark on the physical activity described herein. Since the physical activities described herein may be too sophisticated in nature, it is *essential that a physician be consulted.*

UNIQUE PUBLICATIONS

KUNG-FU
The Way of Life

by DOUGLAS L. WONG

UP UNIQUE PUBLICATIONS

DEDICATION

To dedicated students of this art or any art, may the road of knowledge be forever open to all who seek the truth, for the road of life is a road filled with adventure. May you find the right path to peacefulness and tranquility of the mind. Also to all the past Masters of this timeless art, without their wisdom and foresight this book would have been an impossible task.

I am dedicating this book to one of my instructors who passed away, an instructor who showed me how to live with life and to understand it. He gave me the key to open up the vast knowledge available in this timeless art. An art on Life! As he always stated, "Even when a person dies if someone carries on his teachings and outlook on life he is still alive in body and in soul." "Disseminate a little knowledge to the world, let them understand themselves and the world will be a better place to live."

To my instructor, Mr. Haumea "Tiny" Lefiti, may this book be one that you are proud of. It was written from the heart and given fully the way you would have wanted it. Thank you for the help and love that you gave me, it will always be cherished in the heart as well as in the mind.

Silent Moments

The quietness of silence is felt through the soul
For silence needs no word to explain the sorrow or love within.
Silence is being able to communicate with one's body and mind
The silence of a thought that only thinks of you.
The silent yearning of a desire that won't answer back
The silent surrounding of an empty heart
Leaving a silent person with silent thoughts of a silent life
Breakup the silence of emptiness and let your voice start the silence
Of life back into my heart.
Silence be happy!
Silence don't be sad!
Silence I can help you!
Silence can you hear me?
All is quiet
For the silence of death dwells within my soul.

Douglas Lim Wong
September 1975

FOREWARD

This book was written in hopes of explaining to the many students of this art or any art, the true facets of Kung Fu. This is not a book written to enhance any particular style, but to cover all styles in general. It will explore the theories and concepts of each particular area of involvement.

Kung Fu is one of the oldest fighting art known to mankind. With it come many traditions and customs which are being carried forth today by numerous disciples of each style. Kung Fu is a way of life for many people and it can help ease the tensions and problems caused by today's modern society. This book will expand on the outlook of this relatively unknown art which has been popularized by two phenomena, the "Kung Fu" television series, and by the late martial art hero, Mr. Bruce Lee.

This is a storybook unleashing its wonders and awes to the many knowledge seeking individuals around us. May this book help answer the many questions cluttered within your mind on the art of Kung Fu.

In a man's life there are many goals to accomplish. With the completion of this book I have achieved a milestone of great importance. A step closer to a dream which was but a thought, a thought that turned into a reality, a reality which enhanced my total being both mentally and physically. This book is a summary of the many styles that I was privileged to study. Some styles are relatively unknown while others are very popular throughout China.

This is the first part of my book which will deal with the basics of Kung Fu from the beginning to the intermediate levels. The second book, "Shaolin Fighting — Theories & Concepts" will deal with the higher levels of Kung Fu and will include chapters on the internal system, ranking, breathing, fighting principles and other interested topics. May you use the book to enhance your knowledge of this fabulous art.

Sifu Douglas Wong
Author

ABOUT THE AUTHOR

Sifu Douglas Lim Wong is an individual who enjoys his hobby to the fullest. His interest in this ancient art is one that encompasses the total aspect of Chinese pugilism.

Gung Fu is an art that is timeless, it deals with the events of life and its many consequences. It is a study of life from the day you are born to the day you die. The main branches of studies involved in this art are: Chinese Medicine, Physics, Philosophy, Logic, Psychology, Mathematics, History and also Self-Defense.

With so many subjects involved it is sure that a person must be well versed to ensure the proper teaching of each facet of this art. Also, you must study from a qualified instructor who is willing to share his wealth of knowledge.

He has had the privilege of studying under numerous fine instructors from various systems. He studied under Grandmaster Wong Ark Yuey of Los Angeles, California. Grandmaster Wong is one of the foremost practitioners in the Five Animals Style (Ng Ying Ga), and the Five Family Styles (Ng Ga Kin) as taught in China. At the advanced age of seventy-five years old, Grandmaster Wong is still actively teaching classes everyday. He later studied under Sifu Haumea "Tiny" Lefiti, a senior student of Grandmaster Ark Wong. Sifu Lefiti also studied in Taiwan learning the Mok Ga system and the White Crane system (Bai Hok Pai). He was head of the Polynesian-American Gung Fu Association until his death in 1973. From Si-Hing Walter Wong of Hong Kong, he studied the Wing Chun Chuan system learning the forms as well as the "Sticking Hand Training" known as "Chi Sao."

In 1973 under the tutelage of Master Share Lew, he was introduced to the higher levels of Gung Fu. From Master Lew he learned the Taoist internal system which includes Herbal Medicine, Meditation, and Taoist breathing exercises. Master Lew has been influential on Sifu Wong's knowledge. Master Lew teaches the Tao-on Pai (Tao Ga) system of Gung Fu and also the Choy-Li-Fut system as taught by his late uncle, Grandmaster Lew Ben (Lau Bun), the foremost authority on the Hung Sing Choy-Li-Fut system. Sifu Wong has also been exposed to the Yau Kung Mon style or the "Soft Hand Style," which is a relatively new art which has its origin from the infamous Bai Mei Pai or the forbidden "White Eyebrow Style." Yau Kung Mon was developed in Hong Kong by Grandmaster Ha Hoan. Sifu Wong has also been exposed to Northern Praying Mantis (Bak Tong Long Pai), Northern Sil Lum (Bak Sil Lum), Tai Chi Chuan (Grand Ultimate Fist), Bai Mei Pai (White Eyebrow System) Hsing-Yi Ching (Heart-Mind Boxing) and Bai Fu Pai (White Tiger System). Sifu Wong has also studied the Buddhist internal system and also the Iron Palm training.

From the total teaching of all his instructors he has formulated a new system of his own called the "White Lotus Flower Style" (Bai Ling Fa Pai). The White Lotus represents the purity of this new system among the many styles in existence today. During sunrise the Lotus flower opens up to the world to take in the events of the day. And when sunset approaches the flower closes and is at peace with the world through darkness. The White Lotus Flower is a Buddhist symbol of purity and happiness and has a very colorful history throughout the many eventful Chinese dynasties. Sifu Wong's interest in his heritage and culture was the key that opened the door of wisdom and knowledge to this fabulous art.

Being one of the most respected instructor's on the West Coast tournament circuit. He has produced Gung Fu's "Winningist Team" as quoted from one magazine article. He has achieved many milestones since opening his kwoon (studio) in January of 1973. Since then his Sil Lum Team led and captained by two senior students, Mr. Albert Leong and Mr. James Lew, have successfully captured every notable title in the Kata Division from Junior level to Black Belt level. At many tournaments they have swept every division entered. In Weapons competition they have been the most exciting group to watch. Never letting the people down for a minute, this group has completed and demonstrated throughout the United States and have appeared on many television programs.

Sifu Wong has appeared in numerous movies and television programs, including the "Kung Fu" pilot film from Warner Bros. Studio; "That Man Bolt" from Universal Studio; "Apple Dumpling Gang" from Walt Disney Productions; and other members have appeared on television program such as "Ironside"; "Police Story"; "The Champion"; NBC Sport Show; "Philbin/Brown & Co."; "Sport Prep Show"; "Kung Fu" television series; "Secret of the Martial Arts" NBC series; "Medix" CBS Special; and many upcoming series.

Members have appeared in the Las Vegas Production of "Orient 75" at the Landmark Hotel and also at the Arizona State Fair. They have taken part in many community events and many benefits for underprivileged children foundations.

Sifu Wong has been chosen by Mayor Tom Bradley's Blue Ribbon Committee as the Kung Fu representative for the Martial Arts Advisory Board for the City of Los Angeles. He is also an overseas advisor for the Taiwan based Tang Shou Tao (Kung Fu) Committee of the Taipei Athletics Association.

The Sil Lum members have appeared in magazines such as Black Belt, Karate Illustrated, Official Karate, Oriental Art of Self Defense, Inside Kung-Fu, Los Angeles Free Press, Karate-Ka, Single Register, Combat Magazine from England, Los Angeles Times and many other local newspapers.

Within his Sil Lum Kung Fu school, have been trained such national champions as Albert Leong, James Lew, Robin Kane, Todd Takeuchi and Jimmy Brown, all of whom are known for their hand and weapon form expertise. In the fighting division he has Mr. William Henderson, the reigning U.S. Heavyweight Gung Fu Fighter in full contact matches. He is also one of the more popular fighters on the Karate Tournament circuit.

Assisting Sifu Wong are three long time friends and fellow instructors Sifu Carl Totton, Sifu Tommy Ho and Sifu Wilson Quan. All four of the instructors have trained together at one time or another and have the combined experience of seven different styles of Gung Fu.

This is but a short biography on Sifu Wong, it can only give you a glimpse of his knowledge and his personality. As you read the following chapters in this book you will get a better insight into his personal teaching and a better understanding of this ancient Chinese art.

To my good friend and fellow martial artist — I wish him the best of luck and long life. May this book serve its purpose and help you understand the meaning of life and its many facets.

ERIC LEE

CONTENTS

History of Kung-Fu

Kung Fu, or more properly, Gung Fu, is one of the oldest fighting arts known to mankind. The date of its origins has been lost to antiquity. The term Gung Fu is a term coined by the Chinese who migrated to the United States in the 1800's during the California Gold Rush era and the building of the Transcontinental Railroad. The term Gung Fu means "hard work or task", or "always learning."

The more common term used in China is either "Wu Shu" meaning Martial Art or "Chuan Fa" meaning Fist Fighting. Gung Fu has been practiced and revised in China for over 4,000 years. It has evolved into an implement for health and self-defense. Gung Fu is one of the most complicated and effective systems of self-perservation.

In the beginning of time man came into existence with inborn traits of survival. When confronted with a violent situation, a man can learn to defend himself by using his body, or by picking up an object and converting it into a weapon.

The first punch or kick was considered the forerunner of many of today's fighting systems. From the days of the caveman to modern day society, men have regrouped and trained other human beings in a pre-arranged pattern of self defense. Some styles were used by family members which was kept in their blood line while others taught it in their separate villages or area of living. No two styles were the same because both size and flexibility differed from person to person. Some were tall, short, light, heavy, slow, fast, and some were handicapped by physical injury. (The techniques vary considerably through aging of time due to:

(1) techniques improvement
(2) mixing with other styles
(3) misinterpretation of techniques
(4) undertrained individuals that claim to be masters
(5) deletion through mistrust

It all began, so the legends say, when a stern Indian monk noticed that his young Chinese disciples couldn't stay awake during the long and tiring meditation of the new religion, known as *Chan* or Zen Buddhism, he was trying to teach them. Not conditioned to endure the exhaustive meditative methods developed by the Hindu, Yogic and Buddhist monks of their Master's homeland, the young disciples seemed on the verge of failure in their new undertaking. Realizing this, the first patriarch Bodhidharma took the initiative and introduced his frail disciples to an 18 movement exercise (18 Hand of *Lo-Han*) based on techniques discovered and developed beyond the Himalayas. Soon daily practice of the 18 movements strengthened the young disciples at the Sil Lum Temple enough to receive their Master's teachings thus sowing two seeds that the world would later know as *Chan* (Zen Buddhism) and Sil Lum Kung Fu.

Throughout history credit has been given to Bodhidharma (Dot Mor) as the creator of Sil Lum Kung Fu or the man responsible of introducing the Martial Art ot China. This is not true. Gung Fu was already in existence long before Dot Mor arrived into China. His main contribution was the introduction of *Chan* (Zen) into the Sil Lum Temple.

Nearly 800 years after Dot Mor's death, monk Chueh Yuan, aided by two famous boxers of the time, Li, and Pai, set out to perfect a system which they felt was incomplete.

Upon completion of their work (done within the confines of the. Sil Lum temple at Honan), Ch'ueh, Li and Pai unveiled a 170-movement system, subdivided into five animal styles — Crane, Dragon, Leopard, Snake and Tiger. Known as the Ng Ying Ga (Five Animal Style), they formed complementary styles, each with a different emphasis and approach.

The Crane, based on exercises to strengthen the sinews, stresses balance and quick foot movements; while the Dragon, from exercises for the spirit, stresses flexibility and graceful movement (the Dragon was an imaginary figure but it stresses the flowing spirit of the highly regarded legendary animal. On the other hand, the Leopard, a style that develops power and speed, it differs from the Tiger, a clawing style built on exercises from strengthening the bones. Finally, there was the Snake, based on exercises for *chi* or internal power, and concerned with pin-point hitting of vital spots.

Together, the five animals formed the complete basis of the art of Sil Lum Kung Fu. While countless other styles have sprung from modifications tailored to personal taste or ability, the Five Animals System stands proudly as the complete and original Temple style.

Stretching Exercises

Rigorous stretching exercises were an integral part of the Shaolin monks' daily training routine. Early in the morning, preferably outdoors, they would warm-up with specially designed set of calisthenics meant to extend all parts of the body: joints, muscles, tendons, spinal chord, bones, vital organs, veins and arteries included. Besides developing the flexibility necessary for performing the strenuous Sil Lum forms, the monks were increasing their life expectancy at the same time.

From the earliest of times, longetivity has been the most cherished virtue in the eyes of the Chinese people. A long life meant that one had successfully integrated himself with the ever-flowing Tao; a short life meant failure. Therefore, the primary goal of all Kung Fu systems despite their deadly combat effectiveness was to prolong life. Stretching exercises were intended to enhance one's life expectancy, if they were performed regularly and conscientiously. By keeping the body active and supple which in turn promoted circulation and relieved pressure on the vital organs, stretching guaranteed an abundant lifetime marked by perfect health.

The human body resembles a rubberband. If left inactive, it will contract and soon become stiff and brittle; any sudden or violent motion can cause something to snap, resulting in serious injury. With this in mind, it should be obvious why stretching must not be done haphazardly. Moderation is the key. The exercises must be done slowly at first, getting progressively harder, gradually, step-by-step. The intensity of the exercises should only be increased once the body is flexible enough to withstand the heightened tension without risking unnecessary strains or pulls.

The exercises varied somewhat from temple to temple, depending upon the geography and the prevailing system of Kung-Fu. In the rural North of China, for example, where the rugged terrain is well-suited to a wide open style featuring extended kicks and punches, the calisthenics are more elaborate than in the metropolitan south, where shorter movements and in-fighting were emphasized. Some exercises were to be performed solo; others required a partner or mechanical device. All methods stressed longevity and gradual step-by-step progression.

Nothing is more distressing than seeing an elderly person slowly hobble across a busy street or intersection usually hunched over and relying on a cane for support and only get half way there before the light changes. Due to lack of exercise, their muscles and tendons have contracted to such an extent that they are unable to exceed a snail's pace. Invariably, the mind too, soon becomes feeble. To avoid such a fate later in life, one should immediately begin a comprehensive, sensible, stretching program. Remember moderation is necessary in the beginning, do not try to stretch the muscle so quickly that it will cause an injury. To speed up the healing use the Chinese herbal medicine, Dit Da Jow, in conjunction with a heating device. Do not attempt to over stretch after it heals. The muscles are still tender and need more time to strengthen themselves.

A body that is flexible is a body that can surpass itself in any undertaking. The body that remains supple is able to endure the pressure of everyday living. Keep the body in shape, not merely in tone, but beyond the point of barely making it — you will notice a marked improvement in the body and also harmony with your surrounding environment.

Life is precious and priceless — your body is but a shell surrounding your vital organs. It is up to each individual to shape his own destiny to the optimum potential. Stretch your life by stretching your body and you will be more alert with a relaxed body that is without tension.

(Left) Toe touching: From a standing position.

(Right) Bend forward and touch palms to the ground, keeping the legs straight and feet together. Begin the exercise by touching the toes with fingertips, fore-knuckles and then the palms.

(Left) Grasp the ankle and pull your head toward your knee (front).

(Right) Side view.

(Left) Next try to touch your toes with your elbow. These exercises stretches the upper thigh muscles while toughening the abdominal region. It also expands the back muscles from the neck to the tail bone.

(Left) Drop your body to one side while keeping one leg straight out — both feet should be flat on the ground.

(Left) Lean forward and put your head to your knee. This exercise can also be done by raise the front foot with the top pointed upward.

This lowers the body closer to the ground and is used to stretch the inner thigh muscles and strengthens the ankles. It also develops balance and agility. (Bottom) Side view of above exercise. Remember to switch to opposite side after finishing one exercise.

(Below) Lotus position or pancake. While sitting erect place both feet together, bringing the knee flush to the ground. Also keeping the feet as close to the body as possible.

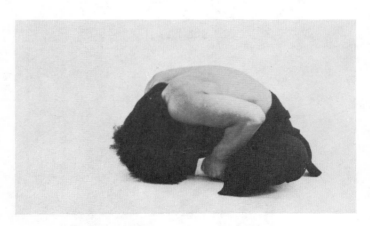

(Above) Side view — bend forward so that the head touches the toe — hold this position from 15-20 seconds in the beginning stage. This stretches the inner thigh and lower back muscles.

(Right) While sitting in the half lotus position prepare to turn to the side by first inhaling.

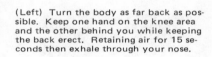

(Left) Turn the body as far back as possible. Keep one hand on the knee area and the other behind you while keeping the back erect. Retaining air for 15 seconds then exhale through your nose.

(Right) Back view — turn neck as far as possible.

(Left) Inhale and turn to opposite direction and hold breath for 15 seconds.

(Right) Back view of above — do this exercise by doing two to the right and then two the left. This exercise forces all the stale air out of the body and replaces it with new air which adds new strength to the body. This also loosens all the back muscles and relaxes the spinal region.

(Below) After finishing the above exercises put both arms out in front and lay your head down flat on the ground.

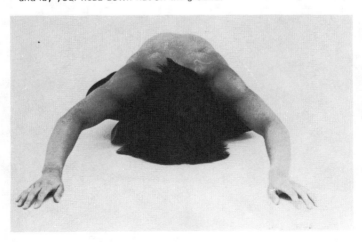

(Left) Now put your head to the right knee cap while trying to keep the head touching the ground.

(Right) Still maintaining the motion continue to opposite knee.

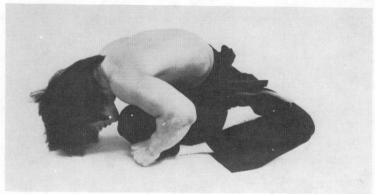

(Below) Side view of exercise. This stretches the muscles of your lower spine and waist region which is necessary for very quick movement.

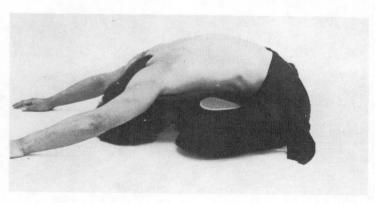

(Right) Stretching snake. Starting position with one leg down with the foot facing inward to the body and the back leg stretched completely out. Make sure the foot is resting on the instep of the back leg. Keep the body erect.

(Left) Start exercising by leaning back as far as possible — stretches muscle in the chest and stomach area — also works by forcing the spine to opposite direction hold position for 15-20 seconds.

(Right) Then lay completely flat with chest and head on the ground — this relieves the pressure off the spinal area.

(Right) Back stretch — sitting erect with both legs straight out.

(Right) Bend forward and put your head on the knee area — try to keep the whole body against the legs. Grasp the bottom of your feet and pull yourself forward. This stretches the muscles from the Achilles Tendon to the spine.

(Right) Next grab the bottom of the foot and pull back as far as possible while trying to lean back — this applies pressure to the outer thigh muscle and works on the arm muscles and back muscles.

(Left) Next turn the toes inward while keeping the leg flat down working on the inner leg muscles and ankle.

(Right) Now reverse process and turn outward and flat.

(Right) Leg straight out — now pull the leg up to the chest region.

(Left) Side view — keeping the body in erect position.

(Left) Now pull the leg up to the ear and maintain position for 20 seconds or more.

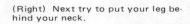

(Right) Next try to put your leg behind your neck.

(Above) Now while still holding the leg drop to the side while maintaining pressure of the leg against the chest.

(Right) Side view — loosen up the hip joints.

(Left) From a seated
position spread both
legs to the side (knee
locked, leg straight),
while keeping the
torso erect.

(Left) Lean forward
with arms spread to
the side until the
chest touches the
ground. This loosens
the hips and stretches
the leg muscles, ankle
and tendons.

(Left) Advance exercises. Sitting in half lotus position.

(Right) Now start to lower yourself slowly while maintaining pressure on the stomach region.

(Right) After landing on the ground place your hand on the ground reverse.

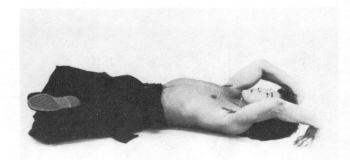

(Left) Push the body upward. This exercise can be done easier if you pull your hand in closer to the shoulder but advances by spreading your hand out further.

(Right) Back bend — regular.

(Right) Advance — now push up on your toe and start to walk toward your head and maintain position for 20 seconds and then walk back to start and repeat.

(Right) In a sitting position place the right leg over the left until the knees are stacked vertically.

(Left) Bend to the left side touching the head to the toe.

(Right) Now rotating to the opposite side. This complex exercises stretches both legs and back muscles entirely. Also if you pull both feet in towards you with the hands it will stretch these areas even more.

(Left) Push both legs out to the side with them both erect.

(Right) Next let your head rest on your knee and lay flat down. Then repeat to opposite direction.

(Left) Body stretch — this is the most difficult and advanced stretching exercise be very careful when performing this exercise.

(Left) Try to touch your head to the toe area and then to the nose and chin area. This stretches the region from the heel to the neck region.

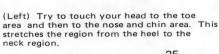

(Left) Begin by placing your leg directly in front of your body with toes pointed straight out.

(Right) Then turn the leg to the side and grab the ankle region. This develops the whole leg using the muscle involved in lifting and turning. This exercise is down slow. Maintain your balance and grace. Do opposite side after you finish.

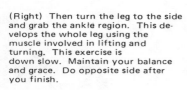

(Left) With the toes pull back and push the leg out with the knee locked and maintaining your balance.

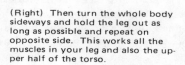

(Right) Then turn the whole body sideways and hold the leg out as long as possible and repeat on opposite side. This works all the muscles in your leg and also the upper half of the torso.

Horse Training

Most Instructors agree that horse riding practice serves a twofold purpose: (1) to develop strength, balance and durability in the legs and lower body (2) and to test the students patience, discipline and sincerity as a prerequisite for advancement to the fundamental self-defense techniques. The term "ma," meaning horse, is like many words in the Chinese language, pictographic in nature. It is immediately obvious to anyone viewing a practitioner poised in the basic "ma pu" or horse stance, that the posture is modeled after a person riding a horse. In ancient times anywhere from the first six months to a year was devoted exclusively to horse training. The students were required to assume the basic posture for progressively longer durations, beginning with the instructor lighting an incense stick leaving the room, and not returning to relieve them until the incense had extinguished itself approximately one hour later. By entering into a meditative state, the monks themselves were able to remain in their "horse" for days on end without moving from the spot for food or water, in a rugged display of mind over matter.

The monks conceived a wide variety of horse stances in addition to the already mentioned each designed with a specific purpose in mind. Some were used to provide a powerful, unyielding foothold; others were used in particular situations, such as: when fighting on a hillside, fighting in water or when pressing the attack.

Each style stressed a certain type of horse. In the Hung-Ga system for example, the emphasis is on a low, very stable posture from which sheer power techniques can be delivered. This owes to the fact that the style was developed on houseboats (junks) in Southern China where a solid foundation was of paramount importance. The Mantis style, with its many hopping and skipping movements, relies on the highly mobile Seven Stars stance with the toe pointed up. Monkey boxing, noted for its fast and agile footwork, employs very low stances which drop the practitioner's center of gravity.

Geography, too, played a key role in determining which particular type of horse was used. In the wide, open and rural North, maneuverability was the primary consideration; so, their horses were designed accordingly. The congested, urban districts of southern China, full of narrow streets and alleyways were ill-suited to the vast sweeping motions of the North. Accordingly, they stressed a more stationary, deeply-rooted stance.

Today many feel that traditional horse training is obsolete. Concerned only with learning self-defense techniques or forms as quickly as possible, they become impatient with instructors who require months of standing in one position. However, by neglecting horse practice they are unable to perform the rapid rising and dropping motions which are an integral part of many Kung-Fu systems.

The horse stances are the foundations of all Kung-Fu movement — a good Gung Fu man can utilize his horse to maneuver in and out of an opponent's range of attack by merely shifting to a different position.

The internal muscle of one's legs are developed to the fullest by using the horse stances as a medium. In Western society there are no exercises for the inner muscle development, they are only concerned with the external or outside surface muscles. Many students that are track stars, football players, etc., can be helped greatly by this type of training. Many individuals after learning this method have recognized remarkable improvements to their speed, coordination and strength.

Many athletics in China are well conditioned because of the ruggedness and time factor allotted on this portion of the training. Before learning to move correctly, it is necessary to know how to stand. That is why the Chinese have a saying that goes something like this. "A person must learn how to crawl before he can walk, walk before he can run, run before he can jump, and think before attempting anything."

Square horse. One of the most basic of all horse stances, the ma-pu or square hourse is found in virtually every style of Kung-Fu. The width of the stance varies from style to style — shoulder width being about the average. When done properly, the back should be perfectly erect and the weight distributed evenly through both legs. This posture is an exact replica of a person riding a horse. The toes may be pointed outward or straight ahead. Knees should be facing outward. Thighs must be parallel to the ground.

(Left) Side horse. This stance is employed when an opponent attacks from the side. The front leg should be bent so that the thigh parallels the ground.

(Right) The rear leg is almost completely extended directly behind the lead leg. In the front view we see that both feet are at a 45 degree angle and the back is straight. Also note that the front knee is turned inward to protect the groin area. Weight distribution: 60% front, 40% rear.

(Left) Cat stance. This low, crouched position becomes an en garde stance using the front leg for kicking, sweeping or transition. The toe of the front leg should be aligned perpendicular to the heel of the rear leg.

(Right) The rear thigh should be parallel to the ground; while the front foot is raised with toes lightly touching round. Weight distribution: 90% rear, 10% front.

(Left 3 pictures) Twisting horse. This stance begins like a square horse, then one leg is crossed in front of the other. It can be used for both attacking and retreating, against single or multiple attackers. The rear leg is kept parallel to the ground with the knee touching the calf of the front leg. Side view. Weight distribution: 70% front, 30% rear.

(Below) Inward horse: used primarily as a defensive position against frontal attacks. The knees are kept just slightly apart so that a blow can't slip into the crotch area. They should bend forward, slightly, with the toes pointing inward at a 45 degree angle and the heels turned outward. Back should remain erect. Weight distribution: even.

(Right) Snake posture: From a square hourse **drop** to either side and slide the opposite leg outward until it is completely extended.

(Left) The back leg remains firmly rooted so that this stance can be used for evasive manuevers or attacking with a surprise leap forward and foot sweep. (Note: don't rely on only one side; always practice horse in both directions.) Weight distribution: 65% rear, 35% front.

SLIDING HORSE. (1) Starting position is a square then by sliding one leg into the other, with both feet together. (2) Side view. Show the knee bent slightly and the weight evenly in both legs.

SEVEN STAR STANCE. Typical stance of the Praying Mantis system. The front leg has its toe upward and resting on the heel. The rear leg supports 70% of the weight of the body. Notice the hand positioning for this style: the Mantis Claw and Hook hand.

From the Monkey system, used primarily for close-range fighting or for pressing the attack on an already grounded opponent.

MONKEY STANCE. This highly compact stance is characteristic of the Monkey Style. It can be used for suprising an opponent with a powerful spinning kick and as a preparatory move for initiating a forward roll and ground techniques.

LEANING HORSE. From the Wing Chun System. This horse is used in side-stepping an opponent's attack. (1) — Front view. (2) — Side view.

CRANE OPEN STANCE. Different from the cat stance because of its high stance and is used to lure opponent into the open area.

(Above) Kneeling horse. One of the most stable of all postures, the kneeling stance allows one to rise or drop quickly with maximum balance and dexterity. The front (right) foot is kept flat with the thigh parallel to the ground. The rear leg is bent with the knee angled inward and down. The heel is raised and the toes touch the ground. Weight distribution: 40% rear, 60% front.

(Above) Crane Stance. Requiring a solid foundation and perfect balance, this is one of the more popular stances in the Crane system. The supporting leg should be angled at 45 degrees and bent slightly for added balance. The top leg is raised knee-high and angles inward to protect the supporting leg and groin. This posture is used for blocking and protecting lower half of the body and for evading leg sweeps. The top leg can also assume an offensive function, namely, kicking.

47

DRAGON DROP. (1) — Side view. (2) Front view — use to drop below an opponent's attack or grab. Drop both legs down with the knee position as in the picture.

DROPPING TWIST HORSE. (1) Ready position, hand outward from each other. Eye to back side.

(2) — Drop the back leg down and start to twist the front leg going to opposite directions. (3) — Complete the twist by dropping into sitting position and hands blocking upward.

48

Body Building

Body building techniques are numerous and vary in method as well as degree. Two of the most beneficial techniques are dynamic tension and isometrics.

Dynamic tension is simply exercising against yourself. Muscle is pitted against muscle, resisting yet yielding at the same time with a scientifically designed series of motions. There is no movement to speak of with isometrics. The principle involves muscle contraction in such a way that there occurs a major increase in tension without a similar increase in length. It is the classic "irresistable force" versus "immovable object" confrontation.

This chapter will be concerned only with exercises for the upper torso — lower body development is related with horse riding practice covered in the chapter on Horse Stances. All are based on proper breathing techniques, muscle control, horse stances and correct mental attitude or awareness.

The exercises are designed to enhance strength, stamina and muscle tone. They are not intended for developing disproportionate muscle size. Therefore, they should be especially attractive to women because they maximize power but not at the expense of femininity. If practiced regularly, they also improve tissues and circulation and keep the veins and arteries cholesterol-free.

Proper breathing methods are essential to these exercises; inadequate respiration will greatly retard improvement. Most people forget that breathing, besides providing oxygen for the blood stream, also exercises the vital internal organs. The main thing to remember is to breath low; center your attention on the lower abdominal region, specifically, a point approximately three inches below the navel. In Chinese Medicine, this portion of the anatomy which is the storehouse for the basic life force — (chi) is called the "tan tien."

Since most Kung-Fu techniques require some form of blocking, striking, grabbing, throwing, joint-immobilization, etc., the upper body must withstand considerable punishment. With this in mind, I have selected exercises that will strengthen the chest, shoulders, neck, back, upper arms, forearms, wrists, and fingers. A note to weight-lifting aficionados — perform these exercises following your workout, and you no longer need sacrifice flexibility for power.

Dynamic tension can utilize every strand of muscle in your body to its fullest potential. The arm exercises strengthens and stretches the muscle from the tip of your fingers to the upper shoulder region. It pulls and stretches the tendons and increases blood circulation, it also provides the development of each and every portion of the upper anatomy.

Power can be doubled or tripled within a short period of time and can be used at anytime without any special equipment. Some can be performed sitting down, others while lying down, and even while watching television or driving. It can be performed any time you have one hand free.

The exercises here are but a few of many practiced at our *kwoon*. However probably the most efficient means of body building comes from applying the theories of dynamic tension and isometrics (to a certain extent) when you are performing a set or "kuen" (kata in Japanese — hyung in Korean). In this manner, every form that you learn can be used to develop power as well as agility, balance, poise and endurance. The slowness also make you aware of what is the correct positioning of the body and it's components as well as which muscle is being utilized.

One final word of caution regarding breathing. Our method is done with the mouth closed, the tongue curled against the roof of the mouth, inhaling and exhaling through the nose. This makes it easier to concentrate air — the "lord of strength" — in the desired location. These exercises will develop what is known as the "hidden strength" in this area of Chinese Kung-Fu.

1a

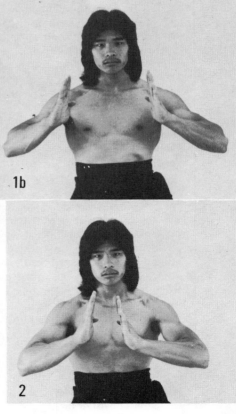

1b

(Above) Circling Palm. Beginning position is in a square horse with arms up away from the body but with the palm facing each other. (Above right) Close-up of hand position. (Right) Push the palm in toward each other while still resisting applying the theory of dynamic tension.

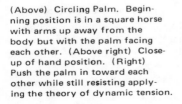

2

3

(Right) Before they come in contact turn the palm outward away from the body. (Below) Push the palm completely out

still maintaining strength on the center of the body.

4

(Right) Separate the arms to about shoulder widths.

5

(Left) Hook the hand downward and (Below right) pull the elbow in towards your ribs —

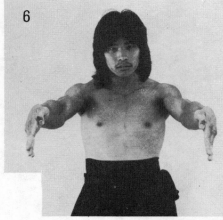

6

then repeat process by turning the hand upward — 10 times.

7

(Above) Punching right hand keep the fist in the center line of the body and maintain pressure while punching straight. (Below) Retain and do the same with opposite hand. Exercise is done slowly and smoothly. Do rep punches to develop the explosive power in your punching.

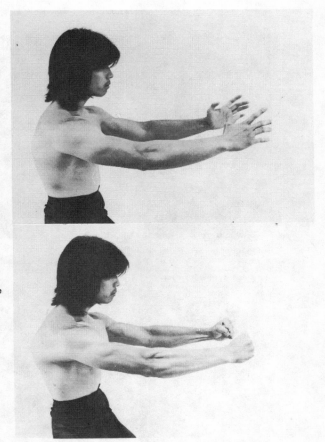

Body is relaxed with fingers open and (Second picture) body is tense with fingers closed. Hold this position for 20-25 seconds and do 15 times. Inhale before exercise and retain breath. Exhale when you relax. Good over all muscle toning for the whole body.

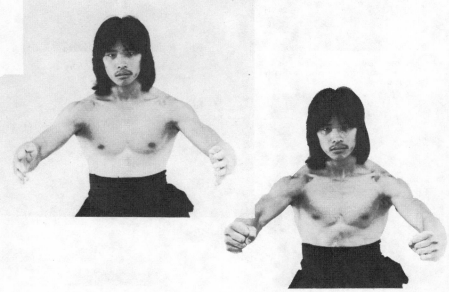

Pushing palm and Hook hand.
Starting position — both palm
in prayer hand position pushing
in hard against each other.

Turn the fingers in toward your
body but not touching the body.

Return to beginning position still
maintaining a continuous steady
motion.

Continue turning the fingers downward as far as possible.

Then back up to starting position.

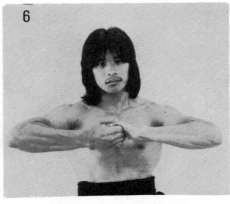

Hook both hands together.

54

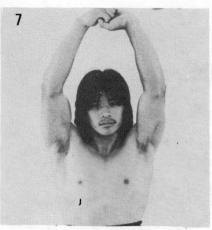

7

Pull the hand laterally while gradually raising the position. Maintaining lateral pressure while going over the head. Be sure to keep the head erect to maximize difficulty, bending forward to lessen the distance is only cheating yourself.

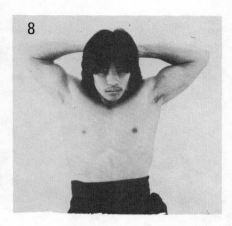

8

Reach all the way back to the base of the neck.

9

Bring it back to the chest area.

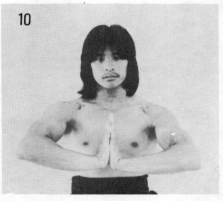

10

Then return to initial position without discipating the pressure. This develops the chest, upper arms, shoulders and forearms.

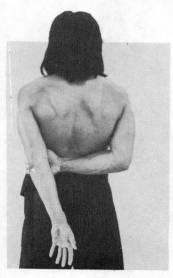

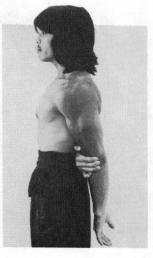

Arm relaxer: with the left arm back — grab with the right hand at the elbow joint and pull laterally in opposite directions. Repeat with right arm. Loosens arms, veins, and arteries after a strenuous workout; develops back muscles as well.

(Left) Square horse position — raise both arms up to shoulder level. Make sure that index fingers are compacted, so that added stress is placed on the forearms. Inhale.

(Right) Begin slowly exhaling as the arms are extended outward laterally. Using the principles of dynamic tension, fight the extension all the way at a steady pace until the arms are completely outstretched.

(Left) Inhale while withdrawing arms half way and turn hand upward to "lifting the heaven" position.

(Right) Extend all the way upward while exhaling.

5

6

(Above) Retract arms down inhaling. (Above right) Exhale while repeating beginning move to "single needle" outward exercise. This exercise develops the shoulders and toughens the veins and arteries, the upper back, forearms and upper arms.

(Above) Finger exercise — assume the Tiger Claw position exerting pressure on the fingertips. Hold for 20-25 seconds. Do 10 set. In both exercises depicted above — inhale and retain breathe while maintaining position. Exhale between sets.

(Left) Side lift. Beginning position — hand at 45 degree angle — fingers together and straight out. (Below) Beginning to lift the arms upward . . . .

1

2

3

4

(Center) Until the back of each hands touch and (Above) return arms downward. (Left) Until finally reaching beginning position. This helps to loosen up the side muscle and stretches out the arms from the shoulders to the fingertips.

5

1

(Left) Pushing exercise. Standing in a square horse put both hands out in front of the body and press the hands together and outward like a spear and hold for 25-30 seconds.

2

(Right) Then put hands behind you and proceed to push both hands inward, this helps to equalize the muscles that are behing used and not to over emphasize any one particular group of muscles at one time.

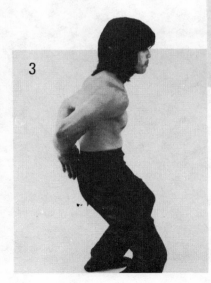

3

Kicking Techniques

Effective kicks are one of the most difficult Kung-Fu techniques, especially for Americans weaned on Western-style boxing. Everyone has probably used their hands as weapons at one time or another; feet fighting, on the other hand, is likely to be less than familiar. So always keep in mind that, although the legs have a much longer reach and are more powerful than the hands, they aren't nearly as flexible and consequently, are harder to maneuver in rapid combination.

Many successful Kung-Fu men have found that the feet are most valuable when employed as a "bothering" tactic, or a means of transition to close the gap between themselves and their opponent. The object is to first stun him with a well-placed kick, then deliver the knockout punch. Few possess the speed, strength and flexibility necessary for dropping an adversary with a kick to the head. The hands play an important role in any kicking situation as follows:

(1) They can be used in a feinting maneuver, to draw an opponent's guard away from an intended area of attack.

(2) They can be employed as a blocking tool while getting into position for a properly executed technique.

(3) They are instrumental in providing balance when positioned on one leg.

(4) When kept low during a kick, they provide the equal and opposite reaction — required by Newton's Third Law which imparts power.

(5) They are essential for any follow-up technique that may be necessary.

There are two prerequisites for effective kicks: (1) strength, and (2) flexibility. Strength is developed through running and "horse" training. Flexibility, of course, comes from stretching not only the leg but the back, waist and hips as well. Sensible body conditioning, footwork (coordination of hands and feet) and timing are important too. A heightened awareness of distance and timing can only come from training against a live, moving opponent.

The Chinese devised many different kinds of kicks to assail the human body, which they divided into three major areas of attack:

(1) the upper gate — comprised of that portion which extends from the face down to the chest

(2) the middle gate — consisting of the heart, solar plexis, stomach and the crotch area

(3) the lower gate — representing the region from the upper thigh to the toes

Techniques like the flying crescent kick and double kick, are delivered while airborne. These are useful against an inexperienced foe and require accurate focus and timing, but, it is usually better to try and maintain contact with Mother Earth. Once you commit yourself in the air, your opponent's mobility and gravity itself are working against you.

High kicks also expose your body to attack — something definitely to be avoided at all costs. Low kicks, delivered to delicate joints, have been shown to be the most efficient and disabling, and are therefore preferred by most Masters. As a rule of thumb, it can be said that Northern styles favor high kicks; whereas Southern styles rely on low kicks, but remember that both styles still have elements from each others kicking arsenal.

The main striking area of Kung Fu kicks includes the entire heel region and the instep. Kung Fu practitioners have found that the heel is most devastating when used for thrusting and smashing as it has the power and weight of the whole leg involved in any attacking situation.

The leg can be the advantage or disadvantage in any fighting situation. Jumping, leaping, hopping, skipping, sliding, shifting, stepping, running, and sweeping are key factors involved in the usages of the almighty legs. The development of each of the mentioned elements can increase your field of mobility and give you an added advantage in any confrontation. Develop both legs when training but when in actual use be prepared to use the best leg forward. Always have your favorite techniques ready for both legs; a techniques which must be capable of striking at different points of the body and also at different angles.

Develop your legs by using different training equipment to sharpen your focus as well as power. Speed is also necessary in your kicks but not as much as timing. The right timing is the most essential element in your attack. Practice with a sparring partner using different types of striking pads in a moving pattern can enhance both mobility and accuracy in conjunction with the timing involved for each strike. More training devices will be discussed in the chapter involving training equipment.

Remember your legs are what takes you to your opponent as well as away from him. Do not rely on your legs alone — your hands are just as important because they are an added advantage for countering many of the kicks thrown at you.

1

2

3

62   (Above) — Combination Kick. Sliding-up Heel Kick and Swing Kick. Ready position.

(Above) Draw the back leg up to the front leg.

(Above) — Snap out the heel into opponent's shin or knee area.

(Above) — Before setting the foot down swing the leg up to an inside swing kick using the whole side of the leg as the striking surface.

(Above) Roundhouse Kick. (1) Ready position. (2) Draw the back leg up to crane stance. (3) Pivot the bottom foot and twist the waist forward and snap the whole leg upward — using the instep as the striking surface (4) Front view.

(Above) Spinning knee lift. (1) Ready position. (2) Draw the knee up with balance on the front leg. (3) Pivot the bottom foot and twist the kick in a circular motion — the height may be varied for different situations.

63

(Right 4 pictures) Sliding up swing kick. (1) Ready position. (2) Drawing back leg up to front leg (3) Twist the body backward. and swing the leg upward. (4) Side View — this kick is used in close-range situations mainly as a checking or agitation tactic.

(Left 4 pictures) Heel thrust. (1) Ready position. (2) Raise back leg up with knee bent. (3) Thrust out straight keeping the knee locked after extending the kick. Work on your balance and make sure the toes are pulled back while kicking with the heel.

(Left 4 pictures). Crane Heel Kick. (1) Ready position. (2) Draw the leg together. (3) Thrust the heel outward making sure the toes are pulled back. (4) Front view. (Note: many Chinese style kicks are delivered with the lead foot, whereas many karate-type kicks are applied with the rear foot. The advantages are that the sliding up and snapping motion is reduced — which enhances speed and the kick is less detectable.

(Above and Right) Twisting heel kick. (1) Ready position. (2) Draw the back leg up and twist the hip. (3) Thrust the heel downward toward knee area. (4) Side View.

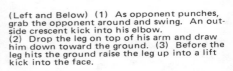

(Left and Below) (1) As opponent punches, grab the opponent around and swing. An outside crescent kick into his elbow.
(2) Drop the leg on top of his arm and draw him down toward the ground. (3) Before the leg hits the ground raise the leg up into a lift kick into the face.

(Above) Crane Kick. (1) Ready position. (2) Draw the front leg straight up. (3) Kick out sideways — using the instep and side of feet is the striking surface.

(Above) Flying Cross Kick. Ready position. (2) Jumping in the air but moving forward. (3) Extension of the kick using the whole foot as the striking surface.

(Left) Inside Crescent Kick. (1) Ready. (2) Swing the leg into a semicircle and hit the side of your foot against the inside of your hand.

(Above) Back Leg Stiff Kick. (1) Ready position — left hand up. (2) Kick straight up and slap down with the left hand. (3) Side view of kick. Make sure your leg is kept straight and knee is locked, not bent.

(Above) Ready position.

(Below) Pull the opponent in and pivot the knee into the opponent's body. The pivot and pulling of the hand doubles the impact power.

(Above) Opponent throws a right punch which is met with a right hand hook and a fore-arm to the elbow joint. Also draw the knee up at the same time.

(Above) Outside Crescent Kick.

(Above) Draw the rear leg up halfway.

(Above) Extend the kick outward past the body. This kick is extremely powerful and gets its name from the circular, crescent shaped motion. The outside part of the foot is the striking area.

(Above) — Cross Kick. Thrust kick with the rear leg, using the heel as the striking surface. Front view of the kick, which should be aimed approximately knee high.

1

(Left) Sliding Up Heel Kick. (1) Ready position. (2) Draw the back leg up to front leg. (3) Snap front leg out with the heel as the main striking area. (4) Front view.

2

3

4

(Above) Ready position.

(Above) The opponent throws a right punch, leans back out of his punching range and applies a cross kick to his knee area.

Ready position.

(Above) The opponent throws a right punch which is blocked with a rising left hand. Draw the back leg in ready for a kick.

(Above) Still maintaining a hold on his hand pivot the body and use a swing kick to the head region. This is an example of a low gate to high gate kicking combination.

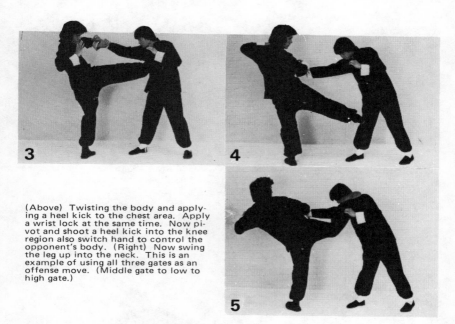

(Above) Twisting the body and applying a heel kick to the chest area. Apply a wrist lock at the same time. Now pivot and shoot a heel kick into the knee region also switch hand to control the opponent's body. (Right) Now swing the leg up into the neck. This is an example of using all three gates as an offense move. (Middle gate to low to high gate.)

(Left) (1) Ready position. (2) The opponent throws a right punch which is blocked and grabbed with your left hand. Apply a back thrust kick to the knee. (3) Now shift the whole weight to the kicking leg and apply an outside crescent kick to the heel.

(Above) — Ready position.

(Above) — Sliding up with a heel kick to the rib — middle gate kick.

(Above) — Ready position.

(Above) — Opponent's punch is met with an inside crescent kick. . . .

(Left) — Ready position.
Opponent punches, grab the punch and apply outside crescent kick to the shoulder joint.

(Above) — Now pivot the leg and use a swing kick to the head — high gate kick.

(Above) — . . . . while still moving turning the kick into a low heel thrust to the knee.

(Above) — Now swing the leg into the face — an example of a three gate kick — middle, low, high.

(Above) — Ready position.
(Above Right) — Block opponent with down hook and raise leg up.
(Right) — Use inside crescent kick to elbow joint.

Kung-Fu Forms

The Chinese forms or sets (*kuen* in Chinese, *kata,* in Japanese, *hyung* in Korean), are the backbone of all Gung Fu styles. Forms were developed by different individuals for various purposes. Some were used mainly as a set of exercises, others for fighting, while some were very simple and others very complicated.

The coordination between the hands and feets in a pre-arranged pattern is of the main importance of form practicing. Forms are used to develop power, grace, endurance, balance, coordination, and as a systematic means of exercising. Also integral to form practice is the mental aspect involved in each and every style. The mind is the key factor involved in all types of physical activities.

A person must learn to adapt to the set he is performing (i.e.: if he is doing a Tiger set he must be strong and ferocious, if a Crane set he must be fluid and graceful). The flowing motion of a Gung Fu set is similar to today's modern dance routines and the traditional ballet of yester-years. But the *kuen* requires more discipline on the body both mentally and physically.

A Gung Fu form is usually introduced by its own particular salute which is relative to it's own style. The salute announces to the audience who you are representing and is used to pay respect to all those around you. There is also an important story behind the development of each and every set. (How it was derived, why, and when and so on). Some sets have very colorful stories behind them while others may have less exciting ones.

In Gung Fu there are standard forms taught in each of the particular styles. The pattern of the form can tell you if it is a true form or a fake. The pattern is very important to the Chinese because they hid many of their secrets in their forms.

Some Gung Fu styles will teach a form three different ways, for example: (Small Cross Set):

Level one — A set is comprised of basic movements with no particularly hard movements. It is taught to beginning students and also to open public classes. It is an introduction to the more sophisticated movements which will be taught at a later stage.

Level Two — The set is composed of more movements that were deleted from the class set. This is usually reserved for the more trustworthy students and disciples. The techniques are explained in more detail and the movements are not as "watered down" as in the first version.

Level Three — The set which is taught only to the immediate family or to the top disciples who have proven themselves to their Sifu. This is the version the instructor practices himself because the most practical moves are left in these sets. They may contain many more difficult moves which only a person of this level can perform, or the set is so easy that only the most useful move are left in. Many wasted moves were put into the level 1 and two forms to confuse the outsiders and to hide its true value.

Not every style goes by this rule. They may teach the same form to all three levels, but the difference is in the explanation of each movement. The combination of certain moves can change a poor technique into a superior fighting technique. This depends on the instructor and how much he trusts his students.

Form training is necessary and a very important step in learning any style. Once a person learns a form and has it explained in detail he is on his way toward learning the core of his particular style. But knowing a hundred forms doesn't necessarily mean you are going to be a good fighter, or a good Gung Fu instructor. It is knowing each and every form well and understanding in detail how each move can be applied and then to change it to fit any situation that may arise which is important.

Each movement has more than one or two usages; an unexpected attack may cause the techniques to be altered slightly or to be re-combined with another one to reinforce the technique.

In form competition, the set is judged on its practical application, focus, power, eye control, breath control, grace, coordination, and the most important of all, balance. An improper weight distribution can cause a form to be thrown off completely and disrupt the whole meaning of the set.

Proper hand positioning, angling, hand usage, and timing are very important to the performer. A misplaced hand, an improper use of one (a Tiger Claw instead of a Crane Beak), can subtract from your score.

Following are a few important points to watch for while performing a set or just watching someone else performing one.

(1) Feet — (the foundation) — are they properly turned in or out to allow. maximum power for the strong moves. The angle of each foot can cut your striking power in half if not properly positioned.

(2) Knee — (lower directional controller) — the knee helps maneuver the legs into the direction you desire. At a certain point it should be bent, at other times they are locked to provide the thrusting power needed to off-balance your adversary. The knee can be either bent forward or leaning back in certain defensive maneuvers.

(3) Thigh — (powerhouse of the legs) controls the rising and dropping movement involved in Gung Fu. The movement must be made smooth and flowing with no sudden jerks or off-balance moves. The thigh can be used in circling your body in a spinning motion to be used as a block or to prepare for a leap or kick.

(4) Waist — (the important gap between the upper and lower torso) the waist controls the whole body and provides the direction with which the two halves can be used to the upmost. This also controls your balance and utilizes the force to maintain a proper weight distribution.

(5) Lower stomach region — (breath and energy controller) proper breathing is important to any activity you may participate in. The breath control centre is the power source of the body. It can increase your endurance or cut your performance in half if done improperly. The breathing is done in the lower stomach area below the navel known as the *tan tien*

in Chinese (the center of your energy source or the power plant of Chi). The center of gravity is also controlled by your breathing. Breathing high in the chest area raises the center of gravity up high, while the lower the breathing the more stable your body will be and better control is easily obtainable.

(6) Back and upper chest area — (the main target involved in an attack situation). The top half of the body controls the body weaving and evasive tactics involved in fighting. The body must be flexible enough to bend in any direction and able to spring back to its original position or into a new one. The chest area in some styles are concaved inward to avoid being kicked while others use the hunchback position. In different forms you can witness the effect of each style of Gung Fu. In the White Eyebrow Style you will notice a hunchback and a caved-in chest area. Also the Mantis Style uses this approach. While in the Tiger Style, the chest region is leaning forward in a side horse position and is considered a very stable and strong stance. The Drunken style will have more of a changing style and is very hard to figure out what the fighter is going to do next. The rolling and tumbling in Gung Fu is also essential in combining all of the movements of the different regions of the body.

(7) Head Region — (the most important part of your anatomy) this region contains the mind which controls your progress and movement; also the eyes, the focusing center of the body. Without proper eye control a form may be out of proportion and can not be performed properly. Your mind controls all the movements and redirects them in the many sequences necessary in a form. The mind must remain calm and uncluttered while going through the set. While performing the form you must become the animal or object being immitated. Let nothing bother the balance or the harmony between your movements and breath. You must be as water running down a riverbed and enjoy the scenery while traveling this unusual route. A person who gets nervous while performing a set cannot unite his mental training into the proper channel.

Remember, a good form can help a person understand his body and what it is capable of doing whether it is mental or physical. An instructor who can not explain each and every move in a logical manner did not learn his sets properly. Beware of those styles which offer you a hundred forms and claim you can master them in a very short time. It's not how many forms you know but how well you know each form.

To understand one's existence
One must understand the reason
For understanding
The understanding process is one
Of many difficulties
It can not be explained in mere
Words and Philosophy
Understanding is an experience
In life
To understand life you must
First learn to live with life.

In the first series Si-Hing Todd Takeuchi is performing
the set as taught traditionally. The second series is performed by Si-Hing James Lew. This method is using the
live hand or the more practical way. This version is used
for more advanced disciples and for fighting purposes.
The traditional method left out many steps while the
fighting method has more destructive moves hidden in
the form. All the numbers are corresponding to each
other (example: showing traditional way, the advanced
form, and the application of the technique.

2

6

7

8

12

13

14

46

47

48

52

53

54

62

65

66

67 **68** **69**

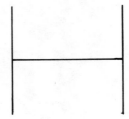

CIRCULAR OR SPHERICAL PATTERN
The continuous form has no particular
sharp angle but encompasses all the direction surrounding your body. This pattern
is the utmost in usefulness and practical application. This pattern is used in
free fighting — a person must be able to
cover any direction at any given time.

H PATTERN
This is the most basic and widely used pat-
tern incorporated by the Japanese and
Korean stylist.

1
2
3

4

5

12

 **14**

 **15**

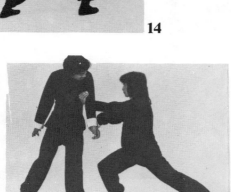

 **18**

 **19**

16

17

20

21

24

25

22

23

26

27

 **28**

 **29**

 **31**

30

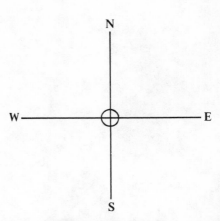

BASIC CHINESE PATTERN
The basic pattern consist of the four direction, East, West, South, and North. The set is usually a very basic set used to teach beginning students.

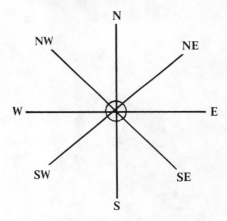

EIGHT DIRECTIONAL PATTERN
This pattern involves more angles which makes it harder to learn but it gives a person more mobility to cover a larger area.

32

33a

33c

34

33b

35

36

37

38

41

42

39

40

43

44

45

48

49

46

47

50

51

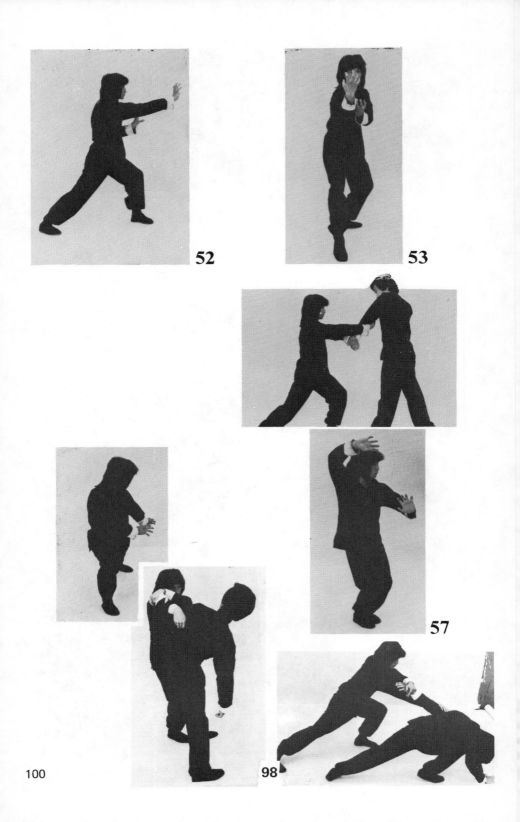

54

55

58

59

99

101

60

61

62

66

67

68

64

65

69

Chinese Weaponry

Chinese weaponry is one of the most difficult phase to learn in the art of Gung Fu. Many schools, and some systems, have abandoned this method o   aching due to lack of proper training or the innability to obtain the   iditional weapons. But, to have a complete background in Gung Fu, one must be familiar with the many types of weapons involved in the art.

The weapons are broken down into many different categories such as long range weapons, short range weapons, soft weapons or linked weapons, double weapons, and throwing weapons (darts, coins, etc.).

105

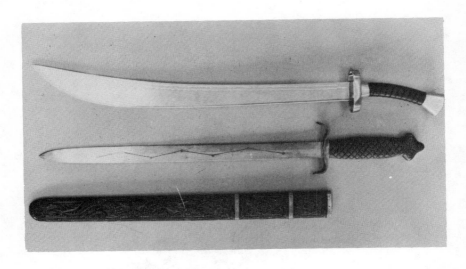

(Above) — PLUM FLOWER SWORD or CRESCENT SWORD also STRAIGHT SWORD

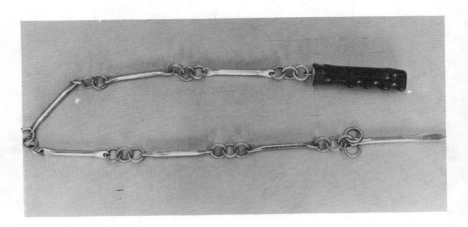

(Above) — 7 LINK STEEL WHIP CHAIN

The weapon training is one that unites the mind and body as one unit since everything must be perfectly in harmony. This prevents injuries not only to your fellow classmates but especially to yourself.

Chinese weaponry has been in existence for many thousands of years, but was systemized when the different founders created different forms or routines to train their students. The weapons are obsolete in today's society, but the training can still be helpful physically, and mentally.

Weaponry teaches you the meaning of control, timing, distance and flexibility. You must know how to handle the weapon in your hand in many different ways, such as blocking, attacking, parrying, maneuvering and evasion.

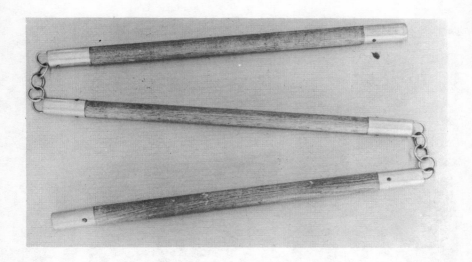

(Above) — THREE SECTIONAL STAFF (Northern China)

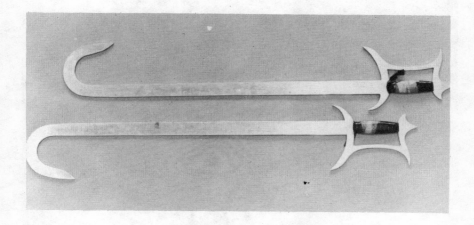

(Above) — DOUBLE TIGER HOOK SWORD (Northern China)

Weapon training improves the student's total art. It includes fighting principles, conditioning, breathing and it is also traditional. Conditioning, precision of movement, and other factors are exercised and strengthened; you have to develop speed, coordination, strength and endurance to perform with weapons.

We study not only the techniques and forms themselves, but we also use different exercises such as dynamic tension and isometrics to develop the hands and arms. We also use different hand forms to develop speed and timing. The weapon froms are done just like the forms (*kata, kuen*) with blocks, parries, attacks, jumps, circling and twisting. The weapons are merely extensions of your hands and arms.

107

One of the oldest weapon in the Chinese arsenal is the wooden staff. This is the oldest weapon used and is considered the father of long range weapon. The staff is usually the first weapon taught to the beginning student in order to prepare him for the more advanced and deadly weapons. The second, but very effective weapon and the King of long weapons, is the Spear. The spear, with its metal point, is very similar to the staff, but it contains the sharpened edge which involves more complicated moves when in combat. The spear is used for blocking other long range weapons but it is never thrown. The Chinese believe that if you throw a spear, you have no weapon left, and your opponent can use your own spear against you. Thus, the Chinese develop a system or form to utilize the weapon to its fullest potential while still being used by both hands.

Another weapon is the Chinese sword or "Gim", the sword is a double edged blade which is straight. This weapon is considered the Queen of Chinese weapons, or the King of short weapons, older than the Gim, however, is the Chinese broad sword, or Cresent sword which is called the "Do" or long knife. The weapon has only one cutting edge and is a very versatile weapon. The Do is considered the Mother of weapons.

There are also weapons which are connected together in some way to give them more flexibility. These are very difficult to handle if you are not versed in this area. This covers such weapons as the three-sectional-staff, the steel chain whip, two-sectional staff, and others like the metor balls which are not too widely known in today's modern society.

There are also weapons used in pairs such as the Butterfly Knives which are strictly a Southern Chinese weapon. Many people consider this the Sifu's favorite weapon. It can be used in close quarter fighting and appears as if you are a whirlwind, or a bird in flight. Another weapon is the Chinese hook sword; this is strictly a Northern Chinese weapon. It is a combination of many weapons rolled into one. It is a combination of the straight sword, sickles, daggers, and when hooked to each other, they expand the radius of safety around you very quickly with a wide effective combat zone.

There are also weapons used for distraction, or for temporarily blinding an opponent in order to land the final blow, or to make good your escape. When fighting more than one opponent, and time calls for evening up the score, there are different darts or coins which can be thrown to lodge into the body of your opponent. Formerly, some were tipped with poison which could kill or paralyze an attacker instantly.

If you should ever witness a demonstration of Chinese weaponry, you will see some of the most graceful movement ever devised for fighting. Most of today's practitioners only practice weaponry as a very graceful dance-like routine to unite their body and mind as one flowing unit. The art must be kept alive to let future generations look at the past. The past which exists today may not exist for the same reason as it was originally conceived but the cultivation of health is still needed.

DAGGER

DOUBLE HANDLE SWORD

BUTTERFLY KNIVES & CASE

DOUBLE DAGGER

A. TIGER FORK
B. SINGLE STAFF
C. TWO SECTIONAL STAFF
D. SINGLE SPEAR

A

B

C

D

A. **SINGLE SWORD** with short tassel
B. **WOODEN TRAINING SWORD**
C. **TAI CHI SINGLE SWORD**
D. **CHINESE BROAD SWORD**
E. **CRESCENT SWORD**

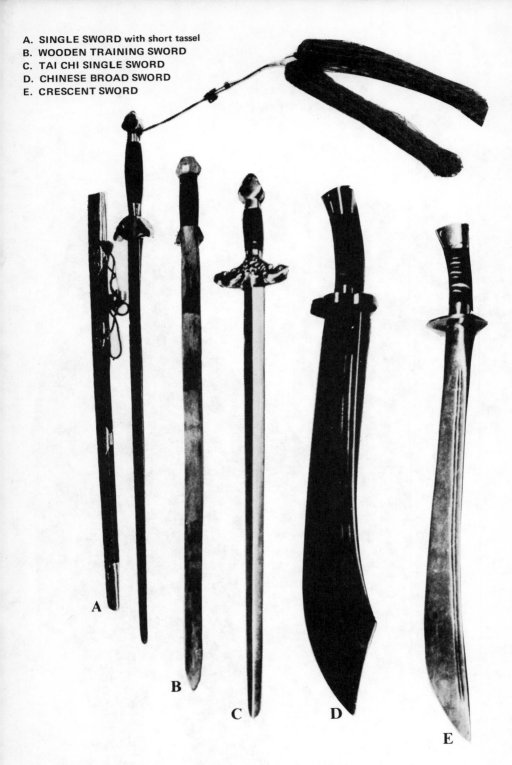